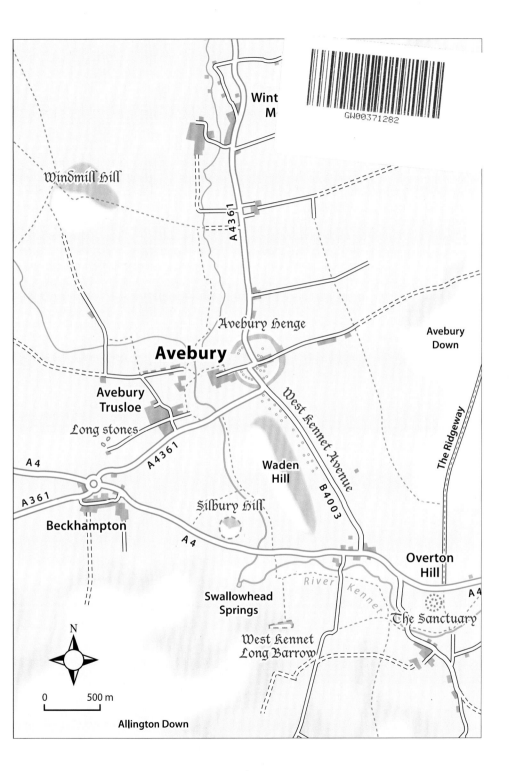

Wint
M

Windmill Hill

A4361

Avebury Henge

Avebury Down

Avebury

Avebury
Trusloe

Long stones

West Kennet Avenue

The Ridgeway

A4361

A 4

Waden
Hill

B4003

A361

Silbury Hill

Beckhampton

A 4

Overton
Hill

A 4

River Kennet

Swallowhead
Springs

The Sanctuary

N

West Kennet
Long Barrow

0   500 m

Allington Down

1

INTRODUCTION

Avebury is not Britain's most well-known stone circle, but being fourteen times the size of Stonehenge it is undoubtedly the greatest.

Situated in the heart of the county of Wiltshire, Avebury is much more than just a stone circle. Within the hundred or so stones that once made up the outer circle were two inner circles each with their own special feature. And, enclosing all of this is a monumental ditch and bank earthwork known as a henge. It has four causewayed entrances and leading from at least two of these were long avenues of paired stones.

If this were not enough, Avebury is deeply connected to the surrounding landscape which has some of the most important prehistoric sites in Britain. Within a radius of just one and a half miles are Windmill Hill, Silbury Hill, West Kennet Long Barrow and the Sanctuary.

Windmill Hill is the site of a five and a half thousand year old settlement contained within a causewayed enclosure, and is located to the north-west of Avebury. The large and mysterious mound of Silbury Hill is probably better known as it can be seen from the busy main road south of Avebury, and is not far from the ancient burial tomb known as West Kennet Long Barrow which lies on the opposite side of the road. And lastly, there is the Sanctuary. This is to the south-east of Avebury and was connected to the stone circle by the longest stone avenue in Britain.

The Southern Gateway

As well as these major sites, there are a multitude of Bronze Age round barrows. All this makes Avebury one of the most complete prehistoric complexes in Europe. Because of its international significance, the Avebury landscape was made a World Heritage Site together with Stonehenge in 1986. The nine square miles it covers contains more than 330 known archaeological sites.

The prehistoric people who built the circles and surrounding monuments were not just concerned with their daily survival but had a culture that could organise these magnificent feats of engineering.

Over the years, many archaeologists have tried to uncover the history of the place. Within recent years, technology has allowed us to

The Ditch

'see' below the ground without digging using geophysical survey with amazing results.

Despite this, more questions are often raised than answered. However, it was obviously an extremely important gathering place. Very little Neolithic domestic rubbish was found here so it is assumed that it was not a dwelling place but more likely used for ritual purposes. It was perhaps a great temple for people who lived in close harmony with their natural environment and ceremonies that related to the seasons and fertility are thought to have been practised here.

Today, visitors come from all over the world. They are able to walk freely between the stones and imagine for themselves the events that took place.

King Charles II was impressed enough by its description to visit Avebury in 1663.

BUILDING AVEBURY

The builders of the Avebury complex did not have the final version of the completed structure in mind when they began. Instead, as with many old buildings, it evolved over a long period of time with new generations modifying and making additions to suit the changing circumstances.

Around five thousand years ago, before the outer circle and great ditch and bank were built, the largest stone in the whole complex was hoisted into position. The stone belongs to the Cove and has been estimated to weigh a hundred tonnes. It has been set very deeply in the ground and is one of the few stones to have remained standing since it was first erected.

The Cove was a setting of three stones set at right angles to each other. The open side was aligned to the north-east; the direction of the summer solstice sunrise. This feature

A henge is the name of a roughly circular earthwork consisting of a ditch with an external bank.

was enclosed by a circle of twenty-seven stones.

Another circle of twenty-nine stones was positioned slightly south of the Cove. This one contained the Obelisk, a single tall stone flanked by an arrangement of much smaller ones.

The two circles became the centrepieces of an even larger circle when a shallow bank and ditch was constructed to define the area. This was the first phase of the earthwork, and was later completely buried when it was decided to increase the ditch's depth to a staggering nine metres (30ft).

The henge measures nearly a mile in circumference and has four causewayed entrances. It is estimated to have taken around one and a half million hours and many generations to accomplish. Digging was done with very basic tools. The chalk was loosened with antler picks and shovelled with the shoulder blades of oxen into wicker baskets. It was then hauled up and deposited to form the bank.

Not only was the ditch twice the depth that it appears today but was also much steeper and narrower. The chalk banks were around five and a half metres (18ft) high and would have been a very striking feature in the green landscape before the grass managed to take hold.

Centuries later, about 4,500 years ago, the outer circle of about a hundred stones, or megaliths as they are often called, were erected inside the ditch.

All the megaliths at Avebury are a local stone called sarsen that were found like natural stepping-stones all over the landscape to the south and east of Avebury thousands of years ago. They can still be seen at Lockeridge Dene near Marlborough where the landscape has been preserved.

The sarsens were not shaped but were chosen for their natural form and fall into one of two categories. Some are tall, rectangular pillars while others are roughly diamond shaped. They are thought to represent the male

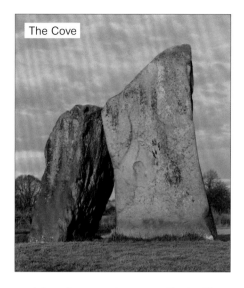

The Cove

and female aspects respectively. They also varied in size with the largest being used for the more important features. The imposing gateway stones, for instance, are considerably larger than most others.

It is thought that suitable sarsens were laboriously dragged to the site on wooden sledges over hills and other

A 'female' diamond and a 'male' pillar standing opposite each other in West Kennet Avenue

obstacles. Once at Avebury, the work had only just begun. Each stone, weighing between ten and a hundred tonnes, was hoisted upright into a specially dug hole, little by little, using wooden levers and straining ropes. Once up, chalk was packed around the base to make it secure. It may have taken many months to manoeuvre just one megalith into position.

Between the outer circle and the Obelisk circle, not far from the southern entrance, a special stone was erected. Although it was not particularly large, it had a naturally formed hole near its top, probably caused by the root of a plant during its formation. At other Neolithic sites, ring stones have been associated with fertility rites.

The final additions were the avenues. Of the four gateways, two are known to have had pairs of stones leading from them. The West Kennet Avenue begins at the southern entrance of the circle and ended at the Sanctuary on Overton Hill. The other led from the western gateway towards

Sarsen's get their name from the Anglo-Saxon words 'sar' meaning troublesome and 'stan' meaning stone.

Beckhampton. Although they appear to snake for miles across the land, they were actually built in short straight sections, and it seems that the stones were paired with male and female shaped stones facing each other.

The building of Avebury took place over a thousand year period signifying how fundamental it was to its people. It seems that observing the movements of the sun and the moon was important to them together with the fertility of the land, their animals and themselves.

What happened next remains a mystery. After a thousand years of intense activity, circumstances changed. Something happened, either locally or in the wider environment, that ultimately led to the abandonment of Avebury.

West Kennet Avenue

Southern Inner Circle

AVEBURY'S DESTRUCTION

The circumstances that led to Avebury's demise are unknown, yet it stood unused for thousands of years. The neglect meant its true purpose was forgotten.

Weather eroded the banks and grass, trees and other vegetation began to reclaim the site. Despite this, most of the stones remained standing and would have been seen by the Romans who were curious enough to visit during their time in Britain between the first and fourth centuries.

During the Middle Ages, the Christian Church became more influential and persuaded the local people that symbols of paganism should be removed.

Whether the people found them

The complete circles would have still been standing in Roman times.

too difficult to destroy or if they feared the retribution of the devil is unclear, as they did not completely remove the stones. Instead they buried them so they could no longer be seen.

The stone had a pit dug beneath it and, after loosening the soil around its base, was pulled down by strong individuals using ropes.

It was at one such occasion that a travelling barber-surgeon was crushed to death. He may have easily lost his footing on the slippery chalk and fallen into the pit just as the stone was falling. Or, maybe as some of the evidence suggests, there is a more sinister explanation. All we know is that he had the tools of his trade with him; they included an iron probe, a hinged pair of scissors and a pouch containing three coins. In the Middle Ages, before surgery had become a profession of its own, surgical tasks were performed by

Avebury's sarsens used in building

In the Middle Ages stones were buried to appease the Church.

barbers who it seemed had the necessary tools.

It was clear that once the stone had fallen there was no benefit in trying to prise it off again. He lay in the grave he helped dig for more than six hundred years until he was discovered in 1938.

The process of burying the stones seemed to come to an end around the time of this tragic episode. Perhaps it terrified the villagers into thinking the devil did have something to say about it after all.

Sarsen is a type of sandstone toughened by silica making it incredibly hard to cut or split. A technique to break them was discovered in the sixteenth century and involved heating the stone in a fire pit, and then, when it was scorching hot, dousing it with cold water. The sudden change in temperature caused the stone to crack. This would be repeated until the pieces were small enough to be useful. It was worth the effort as it was a far more durable building material than the only other local stone available which was soft chalk.

The stone clearing began in earnest in the eighteenth century when farmers profited from selling the stone. It was used in many of the houses and boundary walls in the village. Notice how some of it has reddened from the fire and water process.

It was at the height of this destruction that William Stukeley came upon Avebury and realised it was an important ancient site. Even so, despite

The stone burials stopped after a barber-surgeon was tragically crushed beneath a stone.

his protests the clearance continued. Meanwhile, he produced detailed drawings of the site as it was and recorded stones as they fell. Although the mighty Obelisk was already horizontal before he began, he was witness to its incredible size before it too was broken up for building material.

He also drew the stones of the Beckhampton Avenue before they disappeared. Unfortunately, only two stones of this avenue remain. Known as the Long Stones, they stand in a field near the Beckhampton roundabout.

The years of destruction had taken their toll on the monument. Only fifteen of the original stones were left standing and they were very overgrown and obscured by derelict buildings and farm rubbish. Any visitor would have had trouble realising it was a place of any significance at all.

This was how Alexander Keiller

Stukeley's drawing of a fire pit

saw the site when he arrived in the 1930s. As a keen amateur archaeologist, he planned to return Avebury to its former glory as the greatest stone circle in Britain.

From the 16th century stones were broken up using fire and water and used for building.

The Long Stones. Surviving stones of the Beckhampton Avenue

WILLIAM STUKELEY

William Stukeley was one Britain's first antiquarians. He was also a Fellow of the Royal College of Physicians and an Anglican priest who became particularly interested in Avebury after learning of it from John Aubrey's writings.

William Stukeley

On his arrival in 1719, he was distressed to discover the breaking up of the stones was well under way. He decided that as he could not prevent the destruction he would record as much as possible in drawings before it completely disappeared.

He made visits to Avebury over the next five years recording the positions of the stones in meticulous detail which he later published together with many of his notes in his book 'Abury'.

In his search for detail, he learned a great deal about the stones. It was Stukeley who first observed that larger stones were used for the gateways and other important focal points. He was also the first to notice that the stones had a rough and a smooth side and that it was not coincidence that the 'better' smooth side always faced inwards.

Before Stukeley's time at Avebury, the stones were assumed to have been erected by the Romans because they were the only ones thought capable of the work. But Stukeley rightly supposed that they were much older. He began to speculate on who had created them and why.

As a clergyman, he felt that the organised effort needed to build the circles of earth and stone meant they must have had some religious meaning, perhaps a great temple. He came to the conclusion that it had been constructed by druids because they

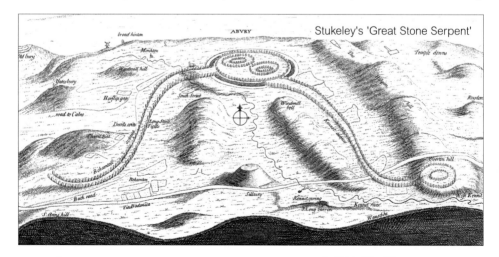

Stukeley's 'Great Stone Serpent'

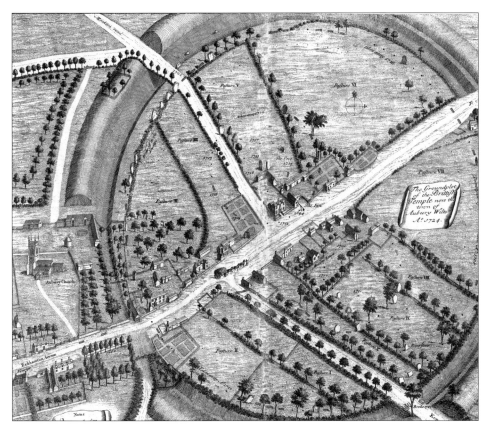

Stukeley's ground plot of Avebury 1724

were the priests of the Celts, who he knew existed before the Romans.

During his later years at Avebury, he became obsessed with druidism eventually seeing himself as the great Archdruid. His drawings became distorted to fit in with his ideas. He came to believe the henge and avenues represented a serpent inscribed in the landscape and he invented the term Dracontia to describe serpent or dragon temples. His contemporaries could no longer take him seriously and as a consequence his work was disregarded by historians for a long time.

More recently though his drawings have helped archaeologists to visualise and understand Avebury's history. Alexander Keiller, who reconstructed part of the circle in the 1930s, was in possession of his sketches and used them to successfully mark the stones' original positions.

They have also proved invaluable to more modern archaeologists in locating features such as the Beckhampton Avenue. For a long time, this was thought to have existed only in Stukeley's imagination as the tail of his 'great stone serpent' but excavations in 1999 proved it to be a reality.

Avebury Manor

ALEXANDER KEILLER

Alexander Keiller was a pioneering archaeologist who first came to the Avebury area in the 1920s. As well as archaeology, he enjoyed skiing, photography and fast cars. He also had an interest in witchcraft and the occult. His extensive work included the excavation of Windmill Hill and West Kennet Avenue before concentrating on the henge and stone circles. He funded the work from his personal fortune inherited from his family's marmalade business. His dream was to return the circles to their original state.

He bought the land and moved from London into Avebury Manor. He employed local labourers to clear the debris, often using dynamite to remove stubborn tree roots. He then set about uncovering the buried stones some of which were over a metre below the surface. Once the original stone holes were located, the megaliths were replaced and securely cemented in. Where the stone could not be found, he used a concrete marker to show its correct position.

It was while removing a buried stone in the south-west quadrant that he discovered the skeleton of the barber-surgeon. His medieval scissors, thought to be the oldest in existence, can be seen in the Keiller Museum along with other finds from his Windmill Hill and Avebury excavations.

Keiller's work became controversial when the villagers learned that his vision of the restored circles meant he intended to remove all the buildings within the henge. Although some inhabitants were

> Alexander Keiller spent £50,000 restoring Avebury.

12

happy to be relocated to a new house at Avebury Trusloe, there were many who resisted the idea of giving up their homes that had been lived in by their families for generations.

Before the onset of the Second World War, which brought his work to an end, he had managed to re-erect fifty stones. His legacy can be seen in the first third of the West Kennet Avenue and the western half of the outer circle. In the south-east quadrant, only the inner Obelisk circle was started.

Yet his time at Avebury has left us with a magnificent monument that would have almost certainly been lost without him. Before he died in 1955, he sold Avebury to the National Trust for £12,000. This figure represented the agricultural value of the land and was only a fraction of the £50,000 he

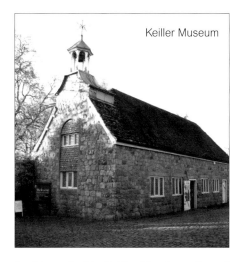

Keiller Museum

had invested in it. The Trust continued with the plan to demolish buildings within the circle, and two-thirds of them were removed before the plan was halted in the 1960s.

The Keiller Museum collection was donated to the National Trust by his fourth wife and can be found in the old stables of his former home.

He sold the land to the National Trust for £12,000.

Stones found and re-erected by Keiller

WALKING TOUR OF THE CIRCLE Approximately 1mile
SOUTH-WEST QUADRANT

Begin in the High Street at the gate to the side of the Henge Shop.

The arc of stones you see before you was restored by Alexander Keiller in the 1930s. Before he arrived, there were only four stones visible out of the twenty-two in this quadrant, and only one of them was still standing. He located the stones that had been buried in medieval times and returned them to their original stone holes.

Where a stone had been broken up and used for building, he positioned a concrete marker over the place where it once stood.

The first stone inside the gate is a damaged survivor of that period. William Stukeley recorded that after it was felled it was taken to the blacksmith's forge to be broken up. It was obviously too much for the man because parts of it were still there

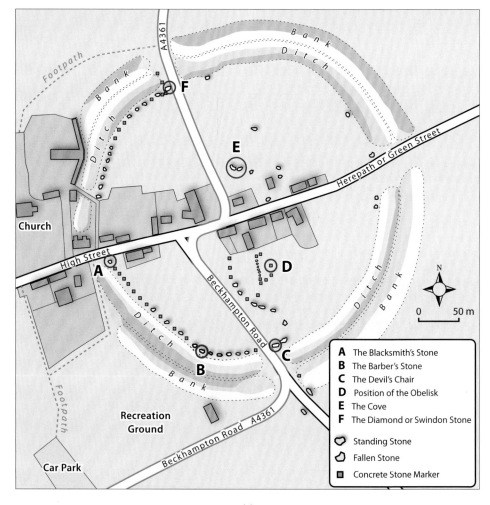

A The Blacksmith's Stone
B The Barber's Stone
C The Devil's Chair
D Position of the Obelisk
E The Cove
F The Diamond or Swindon Stone

Standing Stone
Fallen Stone
Concrete Stone Marker

The Barber's Stone

when Alexander Keiller learnt about it many years later. He recovered what was left and cemented it back together again before returning it to its former position. If you look closely you can see the blacksmith's iron wedge that was used to try and split the stone still jammed near its base.

Further along, you come to the sixth megalith in the arc (not including markers), and this is the stone that crushed the barber-surgeon. It is sobering to think that he lay there for six hundred years in a grave he probably helped to dig. The skeleton was thought to have been lost during World War II bombing, but was later rediscovered in the archives of the Natural History Museum.

Next to the Barber Stone is the megalith that was still standing when Keiller arrived.

Moving on, you will notice a hollow in the bank near to the road. This is not an original feature but damage done

when nineteenth-century road builders dug into it. They used the soil to fill in the far end of the ditch to allow the road to run across it.

After exploring the rest of this section, use the gate to cross the busy road and enter the south-east quadrant.

The Blacksmith's Stone

Concrete markers show where a stone once stood.

SOUTH-EAST QUADRANT

In this quadrant, it may be a little more difficult to make sense of the stone arrangement at first. This is because it was only partially excavated by Keiller before his work came to an end at Avebury. His work concentrated on the inner circle, with the arc of five large stones joined by four concrete markers being the last stones to be restored. Although incomplete, it allows us to imagine the rest of the circle of twenty-nine stones.

At its centre is a large fluted marker that shows where the mighty Obelisk once stood flanked by a setting of much smaller stones. It is believed to have been the tallest standing stone at Avebury and would have towered over two metres (7ft) above the others. It was sadly broken up and used as a building material in the eighteenth century.

Walk parallel to the road towards the ditch and you come to two

The Obelisk stood as the tallest stone of all, and is thought to have been a phallic symbol.

megaliths that form the impressive southern gateway. The stone nearest the road is known as the Devil's Chair and the reason why will become apparent as you turn and look at it from the other side. The natural seat in this stone has been a resting place for countless visitors. They are often surprised, if the weather is wet, as the rain is funnelled down from above onto their heads. This 'chimney', according to local legend, has been said to smoke. Another story tells that the Devil can be summoned by running around the stone anticlockwise a hundred times. There are many Devil stories attached to pagan sites which probably were

The Devil's Chair

The Obelisk

invented through fear of the unknown.

Climb up on to the bank. This will give you a better view of the arrangement and also a chance to see the broken stump of the Ring Stone positioned between the inner and outer circles. When standing, this stone had a natural hole near the top, and at other prehistoric sites ring stones have been connected with fertility rites.

Turn around to look outside the henge and you will see West Kennet Avenue leading over the horizon. The pairs of stones once led all the way to the Sanctuary on Overton Hill, a distance of 1½ miles. It was probably used as a processional way to or from Avebury. Only four of the stones remained standing before Keiller started work. He resurrected a third of the avenue and discovered that the stone shapes were alternate. Male pillars were paired with female diamonds, both next to each other and facing one another. There is a gate to cross the road and explore the avenue if you wish.

Back in the circle, walk all the way around the bank noticing as you do the ridges of eighteenth-century field boundaries. Below the surface of these fields are more stones still buried that Keiller never got to.

Before leaving this quadrant, you will pass a group of beech trees perched upon the end of the bank. Their entangled roots have become exposed allowing us to see the beauty of what would normally be deep underground.

Use the gate to gain access to the north-east quadrant.

Beech Tree Roots

The Cove

NORTH-EAST QUADRANT

The road you have just crossed is likely to have been the main entrance into Avebury in prehistoric times. Green Street, or Herepath to use its older name, leads to the Ridgeway which is one of Britain's oldest roads. The Ridgeway was a high-ground track that connected the Dorset south coast with The Wash in Norfolk and was an important route for travellers in prehistoric times. Avebury's proximity to it is significant.

Today, to come down from the ancient path along this quiet lane is still one of the nicest ways to enter the circle.

> As many as 15 megaliths lie buried in the eastern half of the circle.

Inside the gate on the left is a fallen giant that is one of the eastern gateway stones. It is one of the few megaliths still visible in this quadrant. This is the one sector that Keiller didn't begin to excavate and you can see how little remained. Although it seems like there is not much to see above ground, a geophysical survey was carried out in 2003 which confirmed that there are still as many as fifteen stones lying underground in the eastern side of the circle. The survey clearly defined the size and shape of the megaliths and their original positions, but at present there are no plans to physically re-erect them.

Behind the buildings are two large megaliths standing at right angles to each other. This is the Cove and was once made up of three stones set with the open side facing north-east. This is the direction that the sun rises on the longest day of the year. An outlying stone is thought to have been aligned so its long shadow would penetrate the Cove observing the moment of solstice. This symbolic event indicates that fertility rituals were practised here. If we consider this circle to symbolise the female gender then the Obelisk circle must surely represent the male.

Over the last hundred years, the broader stone of the Cove began to lean to the point where it was in danger of falling. While straightening it, and setting it in concrete to secure its future, it was discovered that it was much larger than previously thought. It extended for another three metres below ground level making it the

Inner Circle Stone

largest megalith in Avebury. Weighing about a hundred tonnes, it is incredible that this was one of the first features of Avebury.

Of the circle of twenty-seven stones that surrounded the Cove, only four are still visible. Two are standing and the other two have fallen.

There is a gate near the Cove to exit this quarter.

The broad Cove stone is the heaviest standing stone in Britain.

The North-East Quadrant

NORTH-WEST QUADRANT

Walking down the footpath alongside the road you come face to face with the Swindon Stone balanced on one of its corners. Although it looks precarious, it is one of the few stones to have remained standing for four and a half thousand years. This is surprising as excavations have shown that its base is not buried very deeply in the ground.

Due to its shape, it is also known as the Diamond Stone and is one half of the northern gateway. The other half was a straighter 'male' stone that was destroyed in the eighteenth century.

Local legend will have you believe that at midnight the Swindon Stone can spin through 360 degrees on its axis, and also that it can cross the road in search of its missing partner.

> The Diamond stone is said to cross the road at midnight to look for its lost partner.

There are three concrete markers here which don't seem to fit in with the pattern of Avebury. They are thought to have been part of a feature that was contemporary with the inner circles and existed before the ditch and bank but, even though some research was done in the 1960s, uncertainty remains.

The inner circle that surrounded the Cove was split by the road and a third of the stones would have stood in this quadrant. The Red Lion public house now covers the position of some of them.

This sector has possibly undergone more change than any of

The Swindon or Diamond Stone

> **The position of some of the Cove circle's stones would have been beneath the Red Lion public house.**

the others. This was the first section of the circle that Keiller tackled due to its poor condition. On Stukeley's eighteenth-century map, it shows an orchard was planted here but a hundred years later it was so thickly overgrown that a person could not walk through it. When Keiller arrived another century later, it was being used as a dumping ground.

After clearing the debris, he discovered eight buried stones and returned them to their sockets. The bank was particularly damaged from the use of explosives to remove tree roots. Consequently, it was remodelled leaving it looking much neater than in the other quadrants.

When the Great Barn was built in the seventeenth century, a large part of the bank was levelled. Although Keiller intended to remove all buildings from the circle, the Great Barn has managed to survive.

When you come to the end of this section, descend the steps. From here you can turn left to return to the shops in the High Street, bringing you back to where you began, or turn right to explore the Alexander Keiller Museum, The Manor, the Great Barn and St James' Church.

> **The bank was remodelled in this quadrant, as dynamite had been used to remove tree roots.**

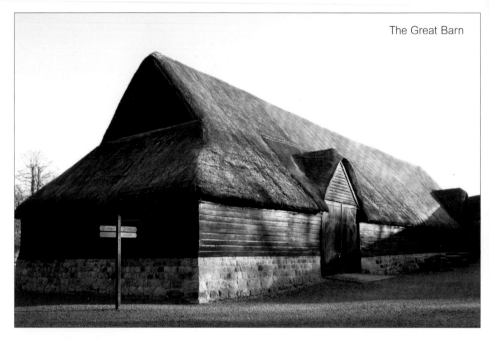
The Great Barn

THE VILLAGE

Avebury Manor

Avebury Manor is a National Trust property that has been the subject of a BBC television series. The house dates back to the sixteenth century and was built on the site of a twelfth-century priory from sarsen and limestone. It has had many different owners who have extended and adapted the house to their needs. The television series followed the restoration of several rooms to four historic periods significant in the house's history. In the 1930s, it became the home of Alexander Keiller and where he established his Morven Institute of Archaeological Research.

Many ghosts are said to haunt the house and grounds. A Royalist from the English Civil War, a beautiful White Lady and a Hooded Monk have all been seen on numerous occasions. Opening hours are restricted.

Alexander Keiller Museum

The museum is situated in the stable block near to the Manor's entrance. It was founded by Keiller while living at the manor to hold his collection of finds from his Windmill Hill and Avebury excavations. Now owned by the National Trust, it provides a fascinating insight into the archaeology of the area.

More exhibits about Avebury can be found in the Wiltshire Heritage Museum in Devizes.

The Great Barn

In the late seventeenth century, part of the henge's bank was destroyed to build this thatched threshing barn which belonged to the Manor. The large doors at either end allowed a horse and full wagon to enter, unload, and leave without having the inconvenience of turning around.

It now houses a National Trust exhibition.

St James' Church

The building can be dated back to before the Norman Conquest in 1066, but has been subjected to numerous alterations since then. The early church was two storeys high and had round windows on the second floor. It is possible to still see three of them in the north wall.

The font is around a thousand years old and was an original feature, although it was an unadorned stone tub at that time. The carving, thought to be two serpents representing evil and sin, were inexpertly carved on it in the twelfth century.

The church is well-known for its rare medieval rood loft. Once used to house a large crucifix, it survived the Reformation by being hidden behind plaster. It remained a secret until 1810 when it was rediscovered and restored.

Many ghosts are said to haunt Avebury Manor and the Red Lion public house.

The Dovecote

The Dovecote

The circular building near the Museum is the Manor's dovecote. In days gone by, the birds were kept to provide fresh meat for the household and made a welcome change to the salted meats that were usually served in the winter months. The birds entered the dovecote through the opening in the roof and used one of the hundreds of nesting holes that line its interior.

St James' Church

The Henge Shop

The Red Lion

The public house is situated on the crossroads at the centre of the stone circle. It is reportedly one of the most haunted pubs in Britain. At night, a ghostly horse-drawn coach has been heard to clatter over the cobbled forecourt. But its most famous ghost is Florrie who was pushed down the well by her husband 300 years ago when he discovered she was unfaithful. The well is now covered with glass and is a feature in the Keiller Room.

The Red Lion

The Henge Shop

This building features on William Stukeley's 1724 map of Avebury. Now the Henge Shop, it is an excellent place for quality gifts, cards and guides. It also has an interesting book section including an extensive range of archaeological publications.

Village Shop

Run by the community, this lively village shop sells a wide range of products from quality local produce to daily essentials.

Chapel & Quiet Garden

This United Reformed chapel was founded in 1670 and built from the circle's broken sarsen stones.

The small garden outside is part of the worldwide Quiet Garden Movement and offers a place for reflection and quiet contemplation.

WINDMILL HILL

The site is approximately 1½ miles north west of Avebury and can be reached on foot by heading west down the High Street. Turn right and follow the footpath continuing on through Bray Street. At the barns, turn right again and follow the track until you reach Windmill Hill.

Alternatively by car, turn right out of the main car park and then take the next right to Avebury Trusloe. Bear left into Bray Street. Turn right opposite the barns. Follow the track up the hill until the road becomes unsuitable. Continue on foot.

It was Windmill Hill that brought the archaeologist Alexander Keiller to Wiltshire. The site is far older than Avebury and was established more than five and a half thousand years ago. It comprises of three irregular rings of ditches and covers an area of about eight and a half hectares (21 acres). It was not a permanent settlement but was a place that people

Seashells and 'foreign' pottery suggest that the people who lived here were traders.

gathered for at least part of every year.

Excavations of the ditches revealed many interesting finds including antler combs, polished stone axes, arrowheads, seashells and many broken pots. Carved chalk fertility symbols were unearthed indicating that rituals were part of life. Amongst all this were human skulls and long bones seemingly discarded with animal bones. And yet, in the outermost ditch, two complete skeletons were discovered of young children. Both were lying on their sides with their heads aligned to the east.

Today, when viewing from ground level the ditches are not very clearly defined. The most evident features are the Bronze Age barrows which are part of a later period.

More information and finds from the site can be found in the Keiller Museum in Avebury and the Wiltshire Heritage Museum in Devizes.

Windmill Hill

SILBURY HILL

Silbury Hill lies approximately one mile south of Avebury and can be reached on foot by the footpath that follows the river opposite the main Avebury car park.

Alternatively by road, turn right out of the main car park and on reaching the roundabout take the first left. Continue until you reach the Silbury Hill car park and viewing area.

As the largest man-made mound in Europe, Silbury Hill has attracted a lot of attention. But after more than two centuries of investigation, it is still reluctant to give up its secrets.

For many years, it was supposed that it was a larger version of a round barrow. These were used for burials, and many of them can be seen

For many years
Silbury Hill was thought
to be a burial mound.

throughout the area. Early antiquarians were known to have plundered them for the grave goods they contained. Because Silbury Hill was so large, it was assumed it was the burial place of a very important person, and would contain the treasures befitting such an individual. One legend says that the golden life-size figures of King Sil and his horse were buried within.

It is no wonder then that three tunnels have been dug into it. The first was in 1776 when the Duke of Northumberland and Colonel Drax hired a team of miners to sink a shaft from the top of the hill. The next was led by Dean Merewether, on behalf of the Archaeological Institute in 1849,

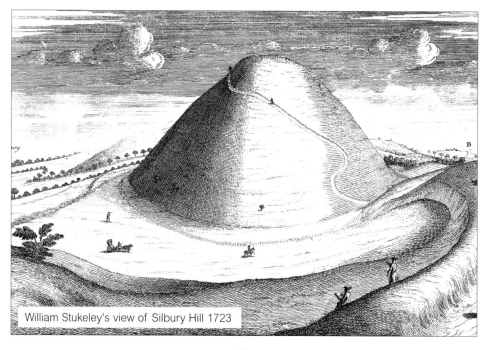

William Stukeley's view of Silbury Hill 1723

who tunnelled in from the side. Lastly, in 1968, the BBC and Cardiff University dug another tunnel running close to the second.

None of these discovered any treasure although the last did uncover important structural details and the remains of antler picks. These were used to date the construction to around 2400 BC.

The hill's base covers more than two hectares (5 acres) and stands approximately thirty-one metres high. It was not simply a pile of chalk but a complex structure built by people with an understanding of soil mechanics.

It began as a small gravel mound which was then covered with soil and turf and surrounded by a ditch. There were many phases of enlargement and each time the ditch was filled and recut. The chalk was built up in circular layers and sarsen boulders were incorporated to keep things in place.

Despite this, after four thousand years, it was in danger of collapsing. In 2000, after heavy rain, a large hole appeared in the top. It was discovered that the first tunnel had not been filled in properly and collapsed into a void below.

Specialist teams were brought in to stabilise it. During the operation, archaeologists had a last chance to record material from inside for future research.

After the complex structural work was completed, all the tunnels and voids were filled which means it should still be standing in another four thousand years. Please note that there is no public access on to the hill.

It was built at around the same time as the Egyptian pyramids.

29

West Kennet Long Barrow from the air

WEST KENNET LONG BARROW

The barrow is approximately 1½ miles south of Avebury. On foot, it can be reached by taking the footpath opposite the main Avebury car park, which follows the course of the river. Cross the A4 and follow the footpath over the water meadow to the top of the hill.

By car, turn right out of the main car park. At the roundabout turn left onto the A4. Just past Silbury Hill there is a lay-by on the right. Continue on foot as above.

On the brow of the hill is one of the longest chambered long barrows in Britain which was constructed more than five and a half thousand years ago. It is possible to enter the tomb where you will find five chambers leading off a central passage.

Originally, there was a semi-circular forecourt in front of the entrance and two ditches flanked the length of the barrow on either side. Now barely noticeable, the ditches were once three metres (10ft) deep and six metres (20ft) wide. The barrow is aligned to the east and its interior would have been illuminated by the early morning sun.

The tomb's use spanned an enormous length of time, until as late as 2000 BC, when for some reason the chambers were filled with earth and rubble and the entrance sealed with large sarsen stones. This is how it stayed until excavations began in 1859 when the western chamber was entered from above by removing the capstone. Later, in 1955, further excavations were carried out and

A local doctor used the bones he found in the barrow to make a medicine for his unsuspecting patients.

30

revealed the passage and side chambers.

The bones of numerous bodies were found in various states of completeness. There were piles of vertebrae, heaps of long bones, bones poked into crevices and lines of skulls set in rows. It is thought that corpses were allowed to decompose then later their bones were rearranged. The long bones and skulls may have been used elsewhere for ritual purposes and then replaced. This made it very difficult to calculate the exact number of bodies found but it is thought to have been about forty-six. These were both male and female and were of all ages from young children to adults.

The stone part of the tomb, made accessible since the excavations, is only about a sixth of the 104 metre (340ft) barrow. It is believed that the remaining part was constructed with wooden chambers that have collapsed over time.

As yet, this part has not been fully excavated, although in the late 1600s a doctor regularly dug into the mound. He had found a good supply of human

Inside the barrow

bones to make, as he put it, 'a noble medicine that relieved many of my distressed neighbours'. His name was Dr Toope, although maybe not surprisingly, he was known locally as Dr Took.

It is interesting to note that many of the bones showed signs of spina bifida and nearly all the adults had arthritis.

West Kennet Long Barrow

THE SANCTUARY

Turn left out of Avebury's main car park. Take the first right onto the B4003 and follow the avenue to the T-junction. Turn left onto the A4 and the Sanctuary is on the right hand side of the road on the brow of the hill opposite the Ridgeway.

Today, the Sanctuary seems unimpressive compared to Avebury's stone circles and Silbury Hill's great size. In 1723, Stukeley recorded it as the remains of two stone circles, one inside the other, before the stones were removed by local farmers.

It was not until 1930, when the site was excavated, that a series of six rings were found. These had held timber posts that predated the stone settings. It seems that around the time the West Kennet Avenue was being built to connect the Sanctuary to Avebury, stones were inserted in-between the posts of one of the rings. The outermost circle was then constructed with stones which neatly incorporated the end of the avenue.

The Sanctuary once had two stone circles, and was connected to Avebury by West Kennet Avenue.

Now nothing is left of the original structures, and its existence is only marked by concrete bricks arranged in concentric circles. The purpose of the construction remains unknown, although many theories have been put forward.

The timber posts may have supported a thatched roof providing shelter for communal tasks. Or it may have been the dwelling of an important member of the community. Another possibility was that it was a mortuary house where bodies could decompose before being interred in one of the barrows. Other suggestions do not see the structure as having a roof, but timber lintels joining the posts together like the stones at Stonehenge.

The stone avenue indicates a processional way either to or from the site, so whatever its purpose, it was obviously a very important part of the Avebury complex.

Prospect of the Temple on Overton Hill. 8 July 1723.

TAB. XXI.

William Stukeley's view of the Sanctuary before the stones were removed 1723